P9-DMM-888

Here We Go 'Round the Year

by Jane Belk Moncure
illustrated by Linda Hohag
and Lori Jacobson

Published by

Mankato, Minnesota

GROLIER

Your partner in education

Distributed by Grolier, Sherman Turnpike
Danbury, Connecticut 06816

The Library — A Magic Castle

Come to the magic castle
When you are growing tall.
Rows upon rows of Word Windows
Line every single wall.
They reach up high,
As high as the sky,
And you want to open them all.
For every time you open one,
A new adventure has begun.

Amy opens a
Word Window.
Here's what she
reads.

Twelve little bears play, "Here
we go 'round the year."

6

"Come and play,"
say the bears.
"Here we go. . . ."

January . . .

brings lots of snow.

Hop on a sled.

Away we go.

February . . .

brings slippery ice.

10

Put on your skates.

The ice is nice.

March . . .

brings a windy sky . . .

just right for helping
kites to fly.

April . . .

brings showers our way.

We make mud pies on a rainy day.

May . . .

brings flowers and butterflies.

June . . .

brings picnics and sunny skies.

July . . .

brings a Fourth of July parade . . .

balloons, ice cream and lemonade.

August...

brings trips to the swimming pool.

September . . .

brings books, pencils and school.

October . . .

brings leaves and . . .

fun-times together.

November . . .

November

brings mittens . . .

and cold, frosty weather.

December . . .

brings sleigh rides,

surprises, and then . . .

a new year begins all over again.

Twelve little bears say, "Can you
read the months of the year?"

How many months are there around the year?